Contents

Safety at home

To stay safe at home there are a few things you need to watch out for.

Take care with hot things

Cookers are **hot**. Dad is using an oven glove so he doesn't burn his hands on the hot cake tin.

What else is hot?

iron

hot drinks

7

Matches are dangerous

Matches
must only be
used by an
adult.

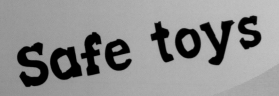

Safe toys

Babies need to play with safe toys.

11

Keep clean

Germs can make you sick.

When should you
wash your hands?

✓ before eating

✓ after using the toilet.

Medicine

When you are ill the doctor may give you medicine to help you get better.

Some medicines look like sweets.
If you take someone else's medicine
it could make you sick.

Be careful with sharp things

Sharp things
can cut you.

17

Keep your family safe

Jack is moving the skipping rope so that Gran won't fall over.

Sockets are dangerous

It's safest not to touch plug sockets at all.

21

Follow the rules

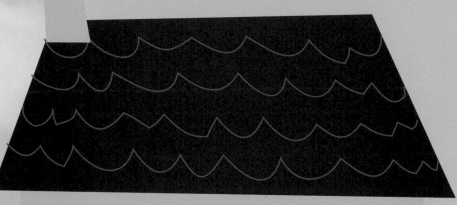

Follow these rules
Make a start
You'll stay safe
And you'll be smart!

23

Index

The end

Notes for adults

Stay Safe! supports young children's knowledge and understanding of the world around them. The four books will help children to connect safely with the ever-expanding world in which they find themselves. The following Early Learning Goals are relevant to this series:
• move with confidence, imagination and in safety
• move with control and co-ordination
• show awareness of space, of themselves and of others
• use a range of small and large equipment
• handle tools, objects, construction and malleable materials safely and with increasing control
• understand what is right, what is wrong, and why
• dress and undress independently and manage their own personal hygiene.

The *Stay Safe!* series will help children to think more about the potential dangers they will face as they grow up. Discussion can be focused on what makes an activity safe or unsafe allowing the children to learn how to protect themselves from harm. The books can be used to help children understand how their own behaviour can make a difference to their safety.

At home will help children extend their vocabulary, as they will hear new words such as *cooker, burn, dangerous, matches, germs, medicine, sharp* and *sockets*.

Follow-up activities
• Show children a group of objects from the home including an iron, cup of liquid, knife, scissors plus a number of harmless objects such as a toy car and a cushion. Ask which objects may be hot and dangerous. Ask which objects may be sharp and dangerous. Do the children know why they may be dangerous? What should they do with them?
• Provide paper and ask the children to draw pictures of what they think germs look like. Explain that germs are actually too small to see. Do they know what germs can do to them? Ask if they know how to help stop germs spreading. Give the children access to a bowl of water and soap and ask them to wash and dry their hands.